Micro Frontends Architecture

Dedicated to my wife Kamini

Author information

For any help and feedback please contact :

Amazon Author Page : amazon.com/author/ajaykumar
Email : ajaycucek@gmail.com , ajaxreso@gmail.com
Linkedin : https://www.linkedin.com/in/ajaycucek
Facebook : https://www.facebook.com/ajaycucek
Youtube :
https://www.youtube.com/channel/UC1uXEebtqCLYxVdzirKZ
GIA
Twitter : https://twitter.com/ajaycucek
Instagram : https://www.instagram.com/ajaycucek/
Skype : ajaycucek
Mobile : +91-7042206393

Table of Contents

Module 1 : Course Overview

Course Overview

Micro Frontends is an upcoming architecture trend which is been lead by the movement towards microservices architecture for backend systems. It's an extension to microservices that realizes all the microservices benefits at the front end part of the your software . This causes an introduction to micro frontend architecture and its design principles. No prior experience with any specific technology or technique is required for this book. Some of the major topics that we will cover includes :

- **Introduction to Micro Frontends**
- **Design Principles**
- **Techniques and Technologies**

And by the end of this book you will know if micro frontends is an architecture style will benefits you in terms of developing cutting edge flexible frontends for both new and legacy systems.

Module 2 : Introduction to Micro Frontends Architecture

Introduction

- Evolution of Software Architecture
- Microservices
- Monolith Frontends
- Law of Diminishing Returns
- Micro Frontends

We will start off this module by looking at the evolution of software architecture of the last couple of decades and how now there is an obvious need for an organisation to adopt micro frontend architecture. We will then lookup how the recent changes in backend architecture in terms of adopting microservices is also highlighted the facts that the similar design principles have to be adopted for frontend systems in the form of micro frontend architecture. We will also lookup the current problems associated with frontend architecture. When frontend architecture ends up being monolithic style where you end up with large front end applications and you will then highlight the diminishing returns from investing in monolith style frontend architecture and then we will conclude the module by looking at what micro frontend are in terms of architecture and how they solve all the problems with the current frontend architecture trends and how also they extends the microservices already done at the backend in terms of software architecture.

Evolution of Software Architecture

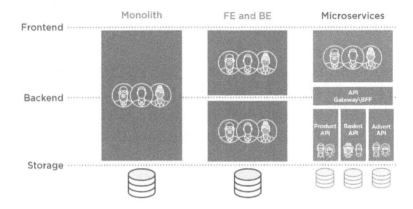

Okay, let's start off with a bit of a history lesson, which will highlight exactly why we have come to a point where we need micro frontends architecture. So software has always consisted of mainly three layers. You have the frontend part of the application, you have the backend, and you have the storage mechanism. The frontend can be in the form of a user interface, which is a mobile app, or it could be a web-based application that you use within a browser, and there can be many other forms, and the backend for your software is normally where the main business logic sits for your software. And obviously storage is where you store all your data that's associated with your application, and it's the place where you retrieve your data from when your software needs it. And in the early days of software development, both the frontend and the backend components would be bundled into one application, which we nowadays call the monolith style of an application. And physically this type of application would live in one code repository, and that one code repository would contain folders dedicated to the frontend parts of the application and folders dedicated to the backend parts of the application, but it would be one large solution that contained both the screens and the business logic, i. e., the frontend and the backend for your entire application, and this entire code base would be maintained by one large team. And because this large monolith contained all the software features that your software provided, changing anything meant that you would have to take the change quite seriously and deployment and testing would be taken quite seriously because of the impact of breaking anything else that's unrelated to the change. The industry then soon realized there's an advantage in splitting the frontend code from the backend code, and at the same time you ended up with a team that specialized in frontend development, and a separate team that specialized in backend development, and this was mainly because people realized that the frontend code and the skillsets required to maintain it had become very specialist, and if you wanted good-looking software, you needed to treat the frontend part of your application as a specialist area that required a team with the dedicated skills. For example, a frontend team that develops web applications will know about all the different intricacies between different browsers and they have the skillset in order to work around those intricacies to provide a consistent experience across all different browsers. And the other reason for splitting up the frontend and the backend part of your application and the teams for your applications was due to the increasing complexity of also the backend systems. Your company's business logic could no longer be wrapped up behind one frontend, and where it's hidden behind that frontend and not available to any other system, we had to treat backend as a bunch of services so that we could share our business logic with other applications in other different forms, and this is why we needed a separate backend team and a backend system, so that we could share our business logic and our business data with the rest of the world using specialist backend skills to develop APIs and services that could share that business data and the business logic. And although things massively improved by splitting up the frontend application from the backend system, and by having two separate dedicated teams, backend systems basically eventually started to suffer from scaling issues. So as the business logic and functionality and data grew, so did the size of the backend systems to support this business logic data and functionality, and at the same time the backend teams also had to grow in size in order to maintain these large backend systems. And when we started to experience that one backend system in the form of services and APIs had to serve multiple different types of frontends in the form of web applications and mobile applications, something had to be done with the backend systems to address the scaling issues. And the solution for backend system was to use microservices architecture to split the large monolith backend applications into smaller services and APIs, each with a clear scope and responsibilities, and each smaller backend system, i. e., each microservice would have a dedicated team that specialized within that service's responsibility in terms of domain knowledge, and therefore, instead of having one large team maintaining a large backend system where loads of code that was coupled together in an unorganized way, we now have dedicated teams maintaining smaller APIs that specialize within a certain area within the business. And the frontend application and the frontend team would call different APIs for different parts of the frontend application, and this might have been done via an API Gateway or a Backend for Frontend API, which spoke to another API downstream within your system. So in the last few years, we all realized that microservices architecture resolves all the backend scaling issue that we were facing for years with the backend systems and the backend teams, and now we've reached a point where we are realizing that we still have issues at the frontend part of our application, in that we still have a monolith frontend application, and we could really do with the microservice design principles that solved all the backend problems at the backend system to solve all the issues within our frontend monolithic application. And this is where micro frontends architecture comes in, because micro frontends architecture is basically microservices design principles applied to the frontend level architecture, and in the next section of the module we will look at what these microservices design principles are, and how they might apply to our frontend layer.

Microservices

- Microservices design principles
  - High cohesion
  - Autonomous
  - Business domain centric
  - Resiliency
  - Observable
  - Automation
- Same advantages for frontend

As it was mentioned in the previous section, micro frontend architecture is basically an extension of the microservices architecture style, and it aims to apply the same design principles as microservices architecture to the frontend part of the software to gain the same advantages that the backend software architecture has had for the last few years using microservices architecture, and therefore, let's quickly recap exactly on what microservices design principles are, and how they might apply to the frontend. So microservices are all about smaller components in the form of services and APIs that have high cohesion, which basically means each service, each API, i. e., each microservice, has one single responsibility and one single focus, i. e., it does one thing and it does it well. And what if our frontend application was also made up of smaller components, each with a single focus. Microservices design principles also suggest that each component, service, or API should also be autonomous. And this basically means each microservice can be independently changed without affecting anything else, i. e., other microservices, and each microservice can be independently deployed, again, without deploying anything else. What if the same was also true for our frontend? Not only is it made up of smaller components, i. e., micro frontends, but each can be deployed independently, and each can be changed independently without affecting any other parts of the UI, i. e., the frontend. Microservices design principles also suggest that each component, API or service are also business domain-centric, and this basically means not only does a microservice have one single focus, but it also represents a specific business domain or business function within the organization. And, again, what if this was also true for our frontend, where our frontend is made up of smaller components, each one relating to a different specific area within the business? Microservices design principles also advocate that each component within your system is resilient, and this basically means even when there is a failure the system is resilient to the failure, and it tries to fail fast, and it tries to embrace the failure by defaulting or degrading the functionality. And, again, what if we had this advantage, i. e., this design principle on our frontend, where if a specific part of our frontend fails, let's say the advert section, instead of failing the entire page, we just silently replace the failed component so that it's invisible to the user that a failure has occurred. Microservices design principles also suggest that each one of our microservices is observable, and this basically means by using centralized logging and centralized monitoring, we can see what each one of our microservices is doing, and we can also monitor the health of that microservice. And, again, what if we had the same advantage at our frontend layer where each micro frontend is transparent in terms of what the user is doing and in terms of what the health is of that micro frontend application. Microservices design principles also suggest that we use automation tools to automate the testing and the deployment of each one of our microservices components. And, again, what if we have the same advantages, i. e., the same design principles at a frontend level, where each one of our micro frontends that make our complete user interface are independently testable using automation tools, and are independently deployable using automation tools? Hopefully from this you can see the advantages our backend systems have enjoyed since microservices architecture style has come into fashion, and also at the same time how these advantages should also be advantages at the frontend level. And in module 3 you will see how micro frontend design principles try and provide the same advantages that the microservices design principles have provided to our backend software.

Monolith Frontends

- Scaling issues
  - Frontend application
  - Frontend team
- Communication issues
  - Multiple teams for one feature change
  - Exhausts time
  - Backend teams are not customer focused
- Code and testing complexity
  - Increased risk
  - Slows continuous delivery
- Advantages of monolith frontends

So in this section of the module, we will look at what can happen to your frontend applications if you choose not to modularize them using something like micro frontends architecture. So over time they will turn into monolith applications, which are harder to maintain, and one of the main issues you will have with your monolith frontend is scaling issues, scaling issues both in terms of the frontend application itself, and also in terms of the frontend team that maintains and develops the application. You'll find that the code base for the frontend application has gotten so large, and the code is so intertwined, making small changes takes a lot longer, and this can happen to any type of frontend application from a modern SPA application that uses a modern JavaScript framework to a server-side type application, which is a web-based server-side application to a mobile application. The frontend code base can get so large that when you have specific performance problems it's hard to scale out that specific part of the application, and you end up scaling out the entire application because there's no other option. A larger code base that's intertwined with different features within the frontend also needs a larger team to maintain that code base, and overall, a large code base with a large team means that every single change will require a lot of coordination within the team for that change to be successful. And overall, these issues result in communication issues, communication slow-down, because when one change is required the product owner has to talk to a larger frontend team and coordinate the communication between the frontend team and the backend teams which maintain all the APIs and services which power the frontend features. And the net result of having to coordinate multiple teams for one simple UI change is is that overall on the project we'll lose time. Another challenge you'll face in this situation is that the priorities of the two teams are very different. The frontend team are very customer-focused because they are close to the UX designs, whereas the backend team are solely focused on optimizing the backend system, and therefore, when you are coordinating changes with the backend team, they might not fully appreciate what you are trying to achieve at the frontend side of things in terms of user experience. Another challenge you'll find with monolithic frontends is, is not only is the code complex, but the testing is also complex, and this is because all the features are intertwined, and changing one feature might result in a negative impact on another feature within your frontend application, therefore overall there is an increased risk of managing this type of monolith frontend. And this increased risk will result in slowed continuous delivery because there will be nervousness around releasing anything because of the risk of breaking something in front of the customer. The only real advantage of having a monolith frontend is that you still only have one single code base, so all the code for all your features is in one pot, and that might ultimately mean that the frontend application is easier to set up for testing and development purposes. And in the next section we'll look at exactly how these advantages diminish over time as your monolith application gets larger and larger.

Law of Diminishing Returns

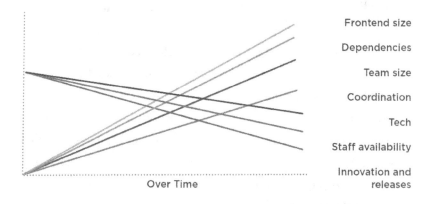

Frontend size

Dependencies

Team size

Coordination

Tech

Staff availability

Innovation and releases

Over Time

So in this section we'll try and visualize what exactly happens as your monolithic application grows in size in terms of code base and in team size. And one of the first things that will happen as your code base increases is that your frontend applications dependencies on internal and external third-party systems and libraries also increases, and again increasing the overall complexity of your application. And to maintain such large complex code base, the size of the team will also need to increase, and as the size of the team increases, the coordination required to make a change to the large code base by that large team, because there are more people involved, the amount of coordination required also increases. And as the ability to change the application becomes slower and slower due to the coordination effort required, the technology frameworks used within the monolithic frontend also become older and more stale, and something that might have been new and fresh at the start of the project will now be stale as the project ages, and as the framework itself ages. And because more coordination is required to change the application, a lot more coordination is required to replace the technologies and the frameworks that the monolithic frontend application initially started off with. And as the tech stack becomes stale that's used by your monolithic frontend, the availability of staff on the market to maintain such application also decreases. There will be fewer and fewer staff that want to work with an application that uses a legacy tech stack. And the net results of having a large code base with a large team that's harder to coordinate with technology that's going stale, and the unavailability of more staff members to maintain that type of large legacy code base, the net result will be that innovation and releases of your frontend application will also slow down, and this is not a healthy situation for any type of business. And in the next section of the module we'll look at how micro frontends architecture can be used to avoid this type of situation.

Micro Frontends

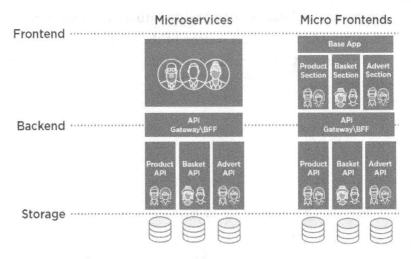

Okay, so micro frontends architecture aims to solve all the problems associated with a monolithic frontend application, and it does this in a similar fashion to the way microservices architecture solves all the problems we had with backend systems, and hence why sometimes micro frontends is referred to as an extension of microservices to the frontend or even sometimes it's known as a microservices websites instead of micro frontends. The approach is very similar in that we take our large application and split it into smaller components. However, there is a lot more to the micro frontend approach than just splitting the application into smaller applications. We are basically trying to make our software completely vertically sliced end-to-end, and this vertical slicing means that our frontend micro frontends are in line with the supporting backend microservices, which support those micro frontend applications, and each vertical slice is basically a feature which is an end-to-end feature. So, for example, within your web app you might have an advert section. That advert section is actually an end-to-end feature in the form of a micro frontend, which is the advert section, and in the background it has a microservice or a number of microservices which support that micro frontend. And this entire feature is owned by one team which supports and maintains and develops this feature end-to-end, which includes the micro frontend application, as well as the supporting microservices in the background and any storage associated with each one of those services. This type of vertical slicing and team ownership of an end-to-end feature means that we inherit now some of the microservices advantages. We can now independently change and deploy a feature end-to-end without affecting the rest of our application. And also if we get specific performance issues we can focus on just scaling out that aspect of our application, i. e., scale out that specific feature with the performance issues. We also now have clear ownership for the features within our application in terms of end-to-end ownership, so we know there's a team responsible for the advert section within our application in terms of the micro frontend, the supporting microservices, and the storage associated with those services, and therefore, within the team we also have improved domain knowledge because they own the whole thing in terms of a feature end-to-end. One of the key aspects of the micro frontend architecture is to give the illusion of one unified application, and not to give away the fact that your one unified application is actually made up of multiple micro frontend. And one of the most common scenarios where you're achieving this is, is to use a base app, which is basically a shell which houses all your micro frontend applications.

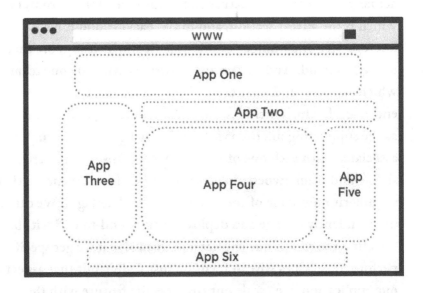

If we now quickly look at an example, an abstract example which shows how micro frontend applications come together to form one unified application, i. e., to give the impression of one unified application, you can see how a base app is used as a shell to contain these micro frontend apps that work together to give the illusion of one unified application. Our single unified application is actually made up of multiple applications which are owned by different teams. These are micro frontend applications, and within the shell, within the base app, within the browser, these applications interact with each other, giving you the illusion of one functioning application that's consistent and coherent. In the next module of this course, we will look at the design principles that you need to implement in order to implement a successful micro frontend architecture.

Summary

- Evolution of Software Architecture
- Microservices
- Monolith Frontends
- Law of Diminishing Returns
- Micro Frontends

Okay, so in this introduction module to micro frontends architecture, we looked at how software has evolved in terms of architecture over the last couple of decades, and we also looked at how microservices architecture has resolved all the issues we've had in the past with backend systems and potentially how the same thinking in the form of micro frontends architecture could solve similar problems within our frontend systems. We then looked at the current trend of building monolith frontend systems, and the disadvantages they bring. And we then looked at how any advantages from using monolith frontends quickly diminish over time. And we then concluded the module by introducing micro frontends, and what micro frontend architecture actually means at a practical level.

Module 3 : Micro Frontend Design Principles

Introduction

- Autonomous Features
- Team Ownership
- Tech Agnostic
- User Experience
- Value Driven
- Microservices Driven

In this module we will look at the design principles that make micro frontend architecture effective
and you will learn micro frontend architecture is actually more than just about splitting up your frontend application into smaller components and we will look at each design principle in detail from why micro frontends need to be autonomous features to why team ownership is important for micro frontend and we will also

look at the advantages and benefits we can get from making a micro frontend applications technology agnostic, we will also look at the user experience and value driven as key design principle for micro frontend architecture and these design principles help emphasize that micro frontend architecture is not all about just technical advantages but it also about the end customer and overall quality of the product. We have already mentioned how micro frontends are extension to the microservices architecture and in this module we will go into more detail in terms of how this affect over all design.

- Autonomous Features
- Team Ownership
- Tech Agnostic
- User Experience
- Value Driven
- Microservices Driven

By the end of this module we know each one of the design principle in detail and we will remind all the design principles for the frontend architecture and different technologies and techniques. In this module we will start off with looking at the first design principle around why micro frontend should be autonomous features and we will cover it in next section.

Autonomous Features

The first design principle we're going to look at is, is the idea around that all our micro frontends should be autonomous features, and by this we mean you might have a web application or a mobile application, for example, which consists of multiple micro frontends within that one application, and each one of those micro frontend applications embedded within your overall application must be an autonomous feature.

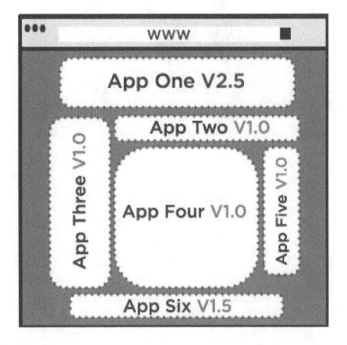

- Independently changeable

And what this means is, that section of your application or your mobile application, i. e., that micro frontend, must be independently changeable from all the other sections, i. e., the other micro frontends within your overall application. And this implies each section of your application, i. e., each micro frontend, should implement business logic top to bottom, so each one of your micro frontends should contain the logic for the UI that it represents, and also the business logic that it contains, and also any database storage related code that it needs or any other code that it requires to interact with services in the background, and all of this should work in an isolated environment for that specific micro frontend. So this basically means your overall application is actually made up of many applications that are end to end that we call micro frontends, and these micro frontends we can independently change without indirectly breaking anything else within our application, i. e., one of our other applications that make up our overall application, so if we break one micro frontend, all our other micro frontends with an application carry on working. This will also allow separate teams within your organization to own each one of these micro frontend applications, and then independently change them and develop them,

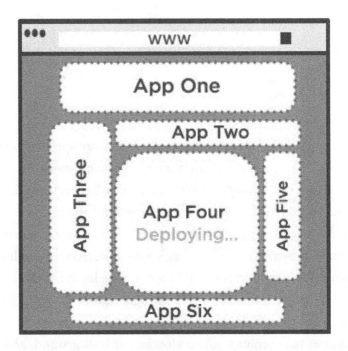

- Independently deployable

and each one of these teams should be able to independently
deploy a micro frontend without having to deploy any of the parts

of your application. Each micro frontend and the team it belongs to should basically be allowed to have its own release cycle so that they can independently deploy an enhancement to that feature at any point.

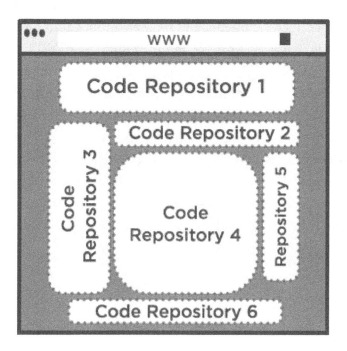

- Code isolation

Each micro frontend also should have code which is isolated from other micro frontends, and therefore you should have techniques and procedures to avoid, for example, shared variables across micro frontends. The idea is each one of our micro frontends can operate independently without accidental or intentional interference from another micro frontend, and for web applications one thing that helps is to use the browser and the DOM as an API instead of using JavaScript code, which ties stuff together in terms of helping your micro frontends interact with each other. Instead, use the browser or the DOM as an API to allow communication between your micro frontends. And if you find two of your micro frontends heavily rely on each other a little bit too much in terms of shared variables, shared functionality, and shared interactions, you could argue that those two separate micro frontends should actually be one micro frontend which features with a new application.

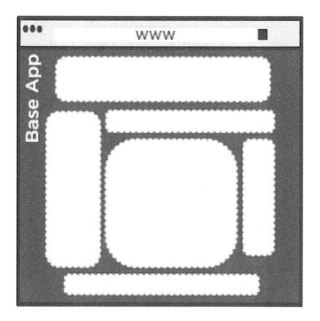

- Base app

And to help with the code isolation of our micro frontends, the concept of having a base application is also important. The base application is basically what houses all your micro frontends into one application. It basically contains the parent DOM where your applications are embedded in a web app example, and in a web app example you could use the base app to share JavaScript, to share CSS, to manage your routing, and to manage the user sessions.

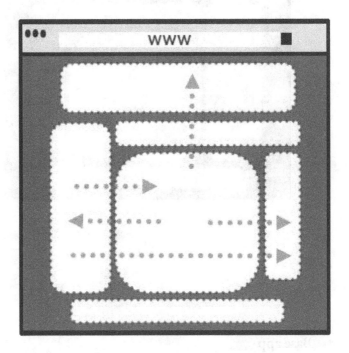

- Simple feature API
  - Communication with other features

The key thing to remember is, although we use the base app for dependencies which are shared, and to keep our dependencies clean so there's no version conflicts between our micro frontends in terms of dependencies, the key thing to remember is each one of our micro frontends must operate as an independent feature, almost like an API that independently operates and has its own inputs and outputs which are independent from everything else. So, for example, like how backend APIs communicate with each other independently in a decoupled way where each API has a RESTful interface that anybody can talk to, each API when it talks to another API doesn't mean that it's coupled with it. Each thing has a decoupled interface which is basically a set of RESTful contracts which suggest exactly how an API can be interacted with without ever knowing anything about the client application, and this is how we want our micro frontends to operate. So what this means is, just because two micro frontends need to talk to each other, we do not physically couple them.

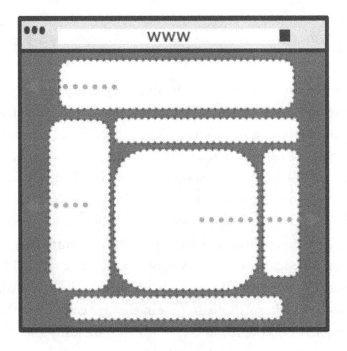

- **Simple feature API**
  - **Communication with base app**

Instead we use our base application, i. e., our browser and our container DOM to raise events that each micro frontend can listen out to.

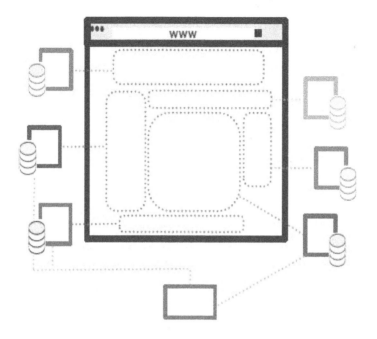

- Simple feature API
  - Communication via microservices

Another way to decouple micro frontends is to have the services that power each micro frontend, i. e., supports each micro frontend, the services in the background also talk to each other, so talk to each other's micro frontend backend services in order to share information, and then render those changes in terms of information on the frontend. This, again, avoids physical decoupling between our micro frontends, because we're using the decoupled microservices architecture to share information between the backend of our micro frontends. Let's quickly look at some visual slides which show exactly how this decoupled communication can happen between micro frontends.

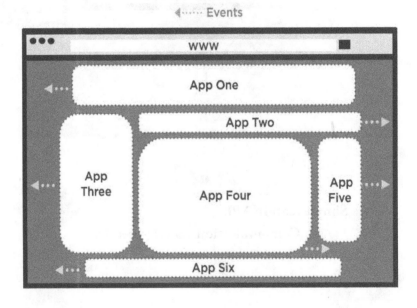

So in this example, when one of our micro frontends need to communicate a change that has happened within itself to the rest of the world, i. e., to the other micro frontends which make up the application, that micro frontend raises an event at DOM or browser level, which the other micro frontends listen out to. For the end user, the experience is the same. They make one change in one part of the application, and the rest of the application updates accordingly, so in terms of experience they notice nothing different.

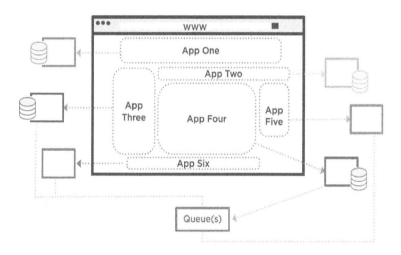

And in the same way we could also use microservices in the background for our micro frontends to communicate with each other, and this, again, allows us to have decoupled communication between the micro frontends because it's the services behind the scenes for each one of the micro frontends that are talking to each other. And this kind of decoupled communication ensures that each one of our micro frontends is an autonomous feature that can be independently changed and independently deployed. And in the next section of the module, we will look at why team ownership is important for our micro frontends architecture.

Team Ownership

- End to end feature owned by a team

Another key design principle for micro frontends architecture is around the idea of an entire team owning a micro frontend end to end, and therefore, in our shopping website example in the product section of our application, the key core micro frontend which is in the middle of the screen, is entirely owned by one team known as the product team, and this product team is responsible for the frontend and the backend and the storage of the data related to the product section of our application. And the same applies to the rest of the application, so the section of our shopping website which shows the adverts, that will be done by the micro frontend team, which are responsible for that specific advert micro frontend, and they will deliver that part of the application as a mini application a as a micro frontend end to end, frontend, backend, and all the relevant storage associated with storing adverts for our shopping website. You could even have a dedicated team which owns the base app which brings all our micro frontends together as a dedicated team that are responsible for maintaining and developing the base app. This will ensure that shared dependencies like shared CSS, shared themes, shared JavaScript, and any other shared component required by our micro frontend within the base application is maintained by a dedicated team.

- Cross functional team
  - Product team
    - Product Micro Frontend -->> API Gateway -->> Product API(s)

And in an ideal situation, each one of these teams and the team members are cross-functional. There's no distinction between frontend developers and backend developers or database specialists. The entire team can contribute to the project end to end. This ensures that the entire team are committed to delivering the micro frontend in terms of functionality, and they have enthusiasm and sympathy for each part of the micro frontend, from the frontend aspects, to the backend aspect, and anything in between.

- Business domain or function
  - Product Team
  - Basket Team
  - Basket Team

This also ensures that the team that owns a specific micro frontend, which represents a specific business domain or function, for example, in a shopping scenario you've got the central product section, you've got the basket, and then you've got the advert section within the application. That specific team that owns that specific area become domain knowledge experts within that area, and over time the teams and specialism and knowledge within that business area will increase, and they can closely work with specific other departments that represent that domain knowledge. For example, on our shopping website, the team that works on the advert micro frontend will over time develop a relationship with the marketing stakeholders within the business, and over time will understand exactly how adverts are more effective within an application due to that relationship, and due to working on that micro frontend end to end over time, and they will gain a more precise specialism within that area.

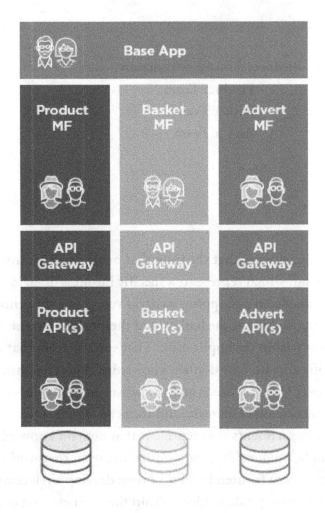

- Focus on one component

This also allows the team to own and focus on one component and optimize that component over time so that it is completely effective within the overall application.

- Advantages
  - Simplifies communication
  - Simplifies coordination
  - Improves agility
  - Improves customer experience

And one of the advantages of having micro frontends owned by a team is that it simplifies communication within your department. So instead of your stakeholders and product owners for a specific area within your application running around talking to different teams, they can talk to one team that can deliver the changes to that feature end to end. Another advantage from end to end team ownership for a micro frontend is that it overall simplifies coordination. For example, if there's a UI change that requires optimization of storage in terms of performance, we can coordinate that effort within the same team because we have a cross-functional team that are enthusiastic about the frontend changes, as well as the backend changes, and we can then coordinate both changes so that we get an optimized result at the UI end. And overall, if there's better communication and coordination within the department, as a company overall this then improves the agility of the company in terms of being competitive. You can make changes more quickly because things are easier to communicate and coordinate. And also overall your customer will experience a better user experience from your application because each component is optimized end to end, so there's no slow backend storage which is slowing any UI elements within your application. And then overall, because your company is also more responsive to change because of the better communication and coordination, your application is likely to change more in line with customer expectations, and is likely to have an edge to provide customers better experience. And in the next section of this module, we'll also look at why it's important for micro frontends to be technology agnostic.

Tech Agnostic

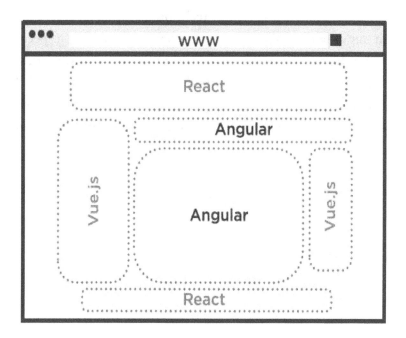

- Tech agnostic

Another key design principle for a micro frontend architecture is that each micro frontend could be technology agnostic. And what this actually means is for our micro frontends architecture that each one of our micro frontend applications should be allowed by the team to choose the right technologies for that micro frontend so our overall application doesn't have to be tied to a specific technology. Instead, for each one of our micro frontends, we can choose a technology that suits that specific problem. And this applies to both the frontend aspect of that micro frontend, as well as the backend and the storage mechanism in the background.

- Future proofing

And allowing this type of flexibility also allows us to future prove our overall application. So instead of investing in one framework or one technology, for example, using Angular for your entire application, and hoping that it won't go out of fashion within the next few years, we can instead say that we are allowed to use any framework for any one of our micro frontends, and then that allows us to be a little bit more future proof in the sense that if one of the frameworks does go out of fashion or becomes technically obsolete, you don't have to replace the entire application, because the entire application is not using one specific framework, instead it's made up of micro frontends that use different technologies, and therefore, as something goes out of fashion, your new additions to your overall application can use newer frameworks within those new micro frontends.

- Right tech

This also allows us to use the right technology for the problem. So, for example, in our shopping website, if the adverts micro frontend requires a slightly lightweight approach, we might choose to use a different JavaScript framework from the rest of the application. And also, for example, if it requires faster storage, we might choose to use a NoSQL database for our adverts instead of using a relational database which might be used by our other micro frontends. So for a specific problem, we can choose the right technology, which gives us optimal performance.

- Avoid retrofitting

Although having technology agnostic micro frontends is a good way of trying new frameworks and moving away from slightly obsoleted frameworks or slightly aging frameworks, I would avoid using micro frontends as a retrofit for legacy applications. Ideally, you want the base application to be designed ground up to support micro frontends, and forcing micro frontends within a legacy monolithic application might cause more problems than it solves.

- Motivates team

Having the ability to choose the right technology and the latest technology for a specific problem, i. e., for a specific micro frontend within your application, will also motivate the team. They will no longer be stuck with or constrained by a technology that's going stale, because for every single micro frontend or every single new micro frontend, they can make the right choice, which not only keeps our technology stack fresh, but it also keeps their career fresh in terms of knowing the right technologies that are in line with current trends.

- Simplification of tech

Overall, by taking this approach, you almost kind of simplify all the technology issues within your department. There's no risk of being stuck to a framework which is likely to go stale, and you can be a little bit more dynamic in terms of what technologies you choose, and, therefore, you are never really constrained by something you've invested in five years ago.

- Not always achievable

However, having truly technology agnostic micro frontends can sometimes be quite a challenge, especially with frontend technologies, web-based frontend technologies,

- Global variables

for example, global variables that are declared in one framework might collide with another variable with the same name in a different framework if both micro frontends live on the same page at the same time so there's an overlap between the two. Later on we will look at technologies that helps separate the runtime where global variables might be less of an issue, but it can be a challenge to avoid them.

- Version conflicts

You can also run into version conflicts where two micro frontends use the same framework but different versions, and that might cause collisions if the runtime within your web app, for example, is shared. As mentioned before, in the final module of this course we'll look at different strategies that allow you to use separate runtimes for your micro frontends so collisions like global variables and version conflicts are less of an issue.

- Library conflicts

And you can run into the same issue with libraries that you use within your micro frontends if, again, everything runs within the same shared runtime if two of your micro frontends use the same library but different versions, you can, again, run into trouble with that conflict in terms of shared variables and version conflicts.

- Convenience of a framework

And because of these challenges, sometimes you will find that it's more convenient to just use one framework for your entire application instead of having micro frontends which are freely developed within any technology that the team thinks is suitable for that specific problem, but there are advantages of sticking to this design principle and then enabling your developers to choose the right technologies for each micro frontend. It gives your overall application longevity in terms of technology, because it's unlikely you're tied to a technology stack that will go stale over time, and instead you can slowly migrate each micro frontend to more modern frameworks as they become available. And in the next section of this module, we'll look at why user experience as a design principle is important for our micro frontends architecture.

User Experience

User experience is also another key design principle for our micro frontends architecture, and basically this is there to ensure that once you gain all the advantages from splitting your monolith frontend into smaller micro frontend applications, you don't completely at the same time ruin the user experience of your application, and this is a risk, especially when micro frontends architecture requires a lot of strategy to implement correctly,

- Performant and fast loading
  - Sensible amount of frameworks

and therefore, by taking account of this key design principle we must make sure that our micro frontend applications are performant and fast loading, and this is especially key for micro frontends because application is now actually loading multiple independent applications that work together in the form of micro frontends, and therefore there might be a lot more going on within the browser when we're rendering the illusion of one application. And this is where we need to be sensible with our technology choices. Although we want the developers to have freedom in terms of what technologies they choose, we still need to be sensible with the amount of frameworks we use. We don't want one application which is made up of a number of micro frontends that each download a heavy framework which is different to the other frameworks within the other micro frontends, overall making our application slow to load and slow to perform. So, for example, in your web application if your web application is made up of, let's say, six micro frontends within one page, do you really need to use Angular for all of them? Could you get away with having some of the micro frontends being static HTML pages that were rendered at server side and then loaded in as a micro frontend, so using a combination of heavy frameworks where they're required and sensible fast techniques where they are sufficient in terms of rendering the content required?

- Corporate identity
  - Base app
  - Style guide vs CSS\JS framework

Another key part of user experience for micro frontends is the corporate identity of your application. Just because you're developing your UI using multiple micro frontends, doesn't mean that in terms of theming, in terms of style, that it looks like a complete mess because everything is inconsistent. And this is where you might choose to use the base app to centralize the styling which is used by all your micro frontend applications. Or instead of centralizing the CSS or the JS frameworks within the base app, you might come up with strict style guides that each one of the teams must abide by when they create their micro frontend applications. Subtle differences between the micro frontends can probably be ignored by the user. There's a well-known shopping website which originally started off selling books, which is quite well-known by everybody, where within their user interfaces you occasionally notice that some of the buttons are not exactly the same. This is probably more than likely because that shopping website is actually using micro frontends within their architecture.

- User interactions
  - Cohesive and responsive UI feedback

User experience also covers the users' interactions with your application, and when the user interacts with your application they want a cohesive and responsive UI which gives them clear feedback. So, for example, if I click the Buy Now button on the central product micro frontend, I expect my cart, the micro frontend which shows the cart on the page to update immediately. So just because I've achieved decoupled communication between my micro frontends, it doesn't give me an excuse to introduce lag in terms of feedback from the UI.

- Fluid work flow

The flow of your application also shouldn't be affected by the fact that you're using micro frontends to make up your application. The application shouldn't feel disjoined, and the seams should be invisible, and there should be no disruption in terms of page-to-page flow. The micro frontends should be invisible within the application.

- Cross browser compatibility
- Consistency across versions

And at a technical level your micro frontend application should work consistently across all browsers and across all browser versions. So the key takeaway from the user experience design principle for micro frontends is that your micro frontend application should not be distinguishable from any other type of web application or mobile application. It should still perform and feel like a consistent, fast, responsive application.

Value Driven

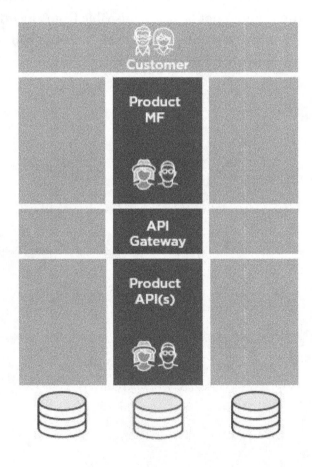

- Each micro frontend is a feature
- Features bring value to the customer
- Entire team can deliver value
- End to end value
- End to end value driven benefits
    - Backend APIs optimized for frontend
    - Data storage optimized for frontend

Another key design principle for our micro frontends architecture is that each one of our micro frontends is value driven, and by value driven we mean that it's a feature that provides customer value to an end customer. And this basically means that there's no point in having a micro frontend which is invisible within your application, and it brings no value to the customer in terms of functionality, and it cannot operate as an end-to-end feature that the end user can use. So, for example, on your web page if there's a requirement for some JavaScript code which keeps track of what the customer is doing within your application or keeps a count of your customers within your application, using your application, there's no point turning frameworks like that into micro frontends, and instead base functionality like that should be part of the base application instead. And if a micro frontend is focused on customer value, the entire team is then working towards bringing value to the customer, which is in line with all the agile principles that we all try and follow. And this also ensures that all changes end to end, i. e., frontend, backend, are all customer value driven and there's no accidental gold plating going on in the background in terms of backend APIs and services. This also makes our overall business more efficient, because each change we make is bringing value to the customer, and we're not making unnecessary background architectural changes which bring no value to the customer. And from a technical point of view, this always ensures that our micro frontend system is always completely optimized to bring customer value in terms of backend API performance, and in terms of data storage performance for our micro frontends. And in addition to micro frontends being customer value driven, in the next section of the module we will look at how micro frontends also need to be microservices driven as they are an extension to the architecture.

Microservices Driven

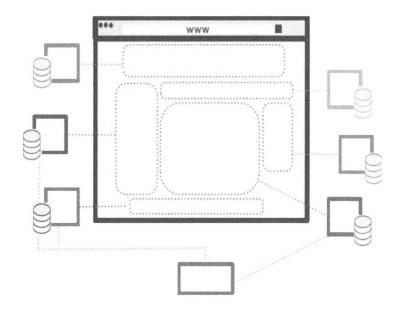

● **Microservices Extension**

Another design principle for the micro frontends architecture is the fact that they are microservices driven. Each micro frontend should have supporting microservices infrastructure in the background to support its functionality. So when we say a micro frontends architecture is a extension to microservices architecture. By this we mean our micro frontends are the front facing components of our background microservices architecture.

- API Gateway or BFF API

So all our micro frontend applications are actually powered by backend microservices and the interface with these backend microservices either through the API gateway or through a backend for frontend API and the sole purpose of the API gateway pattern or BFF API pattern is to provide a frontend application or micro frontend application a gateway to microservices infrastructure in the background

- Bounded context and UI

and now only is the microservices architecture good in terms of supporting our micro frontend applications as backend architecture but also some of the concepts for microservices architecture can be use to define the scope for our micro frontend applications. So what features within our micro frontend application is UI driven but it also can be driven by microservice technique like bounded context to define exactly whats included within the micro frontend in terms of functionality and a bounded context can be used to avoid scope creep of our micro frontend in terms of functionality

- Modular

And by combining both architecture, we are ensuring an architecture which has modular backend and because microservices architecture is key to the success to the micro frontends architecture its important that you understand the design principles and the design patterns associated microservices.

Summary

- Autonomous Features
- Team Ownership
- Tech Agnostic
- User Experience
- Value Driven
- Microservices Driven

Okay, so in this module we learned the key design principles that we want to achieve for our micro frontends architecture. We learned how we want our micro frontend applications to be autonomous features that can be independently changed and independently deployed. We also looked at the importance of a team owning a micro frontend end to end, from the frontend part of the application, either micro frontend to the backend services, microservices which support the micro frontend application. We also looked at the advantages of having our micro frontends not tied to a technology standard, giving the team the opportunity to choose the right technology for the problem they are trying to solve with the micro frontend application. We also looked at the importance of user experience for our micro frontend architecture application, both in terms of UI performance and in terms of UI consistency. We also looked at how micro frontends should not be technically driven, but driven in terms of customer value. Each micro frontend's purpose should be to provide functionality to the user, and that should be seen through end to end within the micro frontend. And we then concluded the module by looking at how micro frontend architecture is not only inspired by microservices architecture, but it's also powered by microservices in the background in terms of your micro frontend applications. Each micro frontend application should have supporting microservices in the background that facilitate its functionality. And in the next module of this course, we will use these design principles to assess different techniques and technologies that allow us to implement micro frontends architecture.

Module 4 : Micro Frontend Techniques and Technologies

Introduction

- ➤ Micro Frontends
  - ○ Shared Runtime
    - ■ Web Components
    - ■ Framework Based Components
    - ■ Transclusion
  - ○ Separate Runtime
    - ■ Micro Apps
    - ■ Iframes

In this module we will look at the techniques and technologies which enable us to develop micro frontends architecture. We will start off by looking at the techniques and technology which falls under category Separate Runtime and Separate Runtime type micro frontend applications allow you to create micro frontend applications that completely independent of each other in terms of process that do not share memory and therefore you get less conflicts in terms conflicting and overlapping variables between your micro frontends. In this category we will start off by looking at Micro Apps and then iframes as a technology that can be used to deliver micro frontend applications and then in the second half of the module we look at the another approach to micro frontends architecture which involves using techniques and technologies which which falls in the category of shared runtime basically allow you to create micro frontend applications that work within the same process and therefor share memory and this means the challenges presented by this approach are slightly different to micro frontend which run in separate runtime. Challenges like sharing resources and sharing memory and the conflicts between the versions of frameworks and then conflicts between overlapping variables. In this category we will see web components as a technology that can enable the micro frontends then we will see framework based components as an approach to micro frontends architecture and then we conclude module by looking at transclusion as technique to develop micro frontends architecture. During this module we will use the micro frontends architecture design principles that we have covered in previous module.

➤ Autonomous Features
➤ Team Ownership
➤ Tech Agnostic
➤ User Experience
➤ Value Driven
➤ Microservice Driven

Micro Apps

Okay, so the first technique we're going to look at, which will enable us to create micro frontend applications, is something known as micro apps. And as previously mentioned, this allows us to create micro frontend applications that run in complete isolation, i. e., separate runtimes.

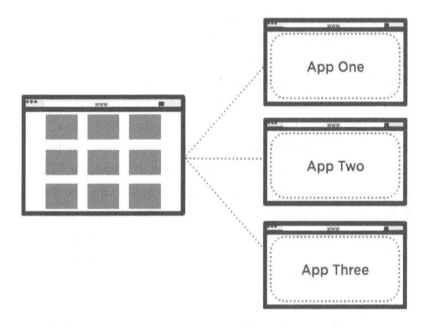

And this is because micro app micro frontend applications are actually independent applications that are completely developed independently from each other, and this diagram tries to illustrate how this might work in a web app situation, and each one of your micro frontend applications is actually a miniature application that is an independent application. And the illusion of having one application is given by having links between the applications, so each link within our micro frontend application instead of taking you to another page within that micro frontend application, it instead takes you to another micro frontend micro application. And to further reinforce the illusion of having one application, your micro apps will have a consistent UI in terms of a shared theme, shared style, and shared UI resources, which give the illusion of one application. And these UI resources, themes, and styles, might be centrally available to all your web applications in the form of a centralized CDN, and also in a SPA application situation, each one of these micro apps will actually be an individual SPA that has links to a different micro app, a different SPA, which when you click on the link it actually loads a completely different SPA within your browser. And by having shared generic UI controls, in the form of, for example, SPA components, you can have specific components that are shared across all your micro apps to, again, give that consistent illusion of one application. So, for example, if each one of your applications needs to feature the same navigation control, the navigation control can be in the form of a shared component, in the form of a shared SPA generic component that can be embedded within each one of our micro apps, again, to give that illusion of having one application. And these shared components, these shared UI generic components will need to be maintained in that way long term to avoid unnecessary decoupling to specific scenarios within one specific application. And to further reinforce the illusion of one application, you could also have a single sign-on mechanism, which once you're logged into one of the applications, or if you're logged into a dashboard, you're logged into all the applications because you've logged in once, and all the applications use the same authentication server to validate the same credentials once you've logged in. And this will ensure overall, that when your user is jumping between the micro applications they are never faced again with the login page once they've logged in to the main application, to the main dashboard or to a specific application. So the illusion is maintained that you're actually still navigating within the one application, because you never see the login screen again once you've logged in.

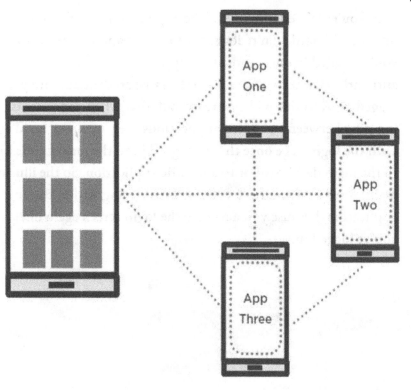

The same approach can be taken with mobile applications, where when you're within one micro application it allows you to jump into another mobile application, which is basically another micro app which is part of your ecosystem. However, trying to maintain the illusion of one application in a mobile application situation might be a little bit more challenging to achieve, and different mobile operating systems will present different challenges. For example, some might make it more apparent that you're jumping between different applications, and the ability to jump back to an application might be even more apparent or even more challenging.

- ➤ Autonomous Features ✔
- ➤ Team Ownership ✔
- ➤ Tech Agnostic ✔
- ➤ User Experience ✘
- ➤ Value Driven ✔
- ➤ Microservice Driven ✔

Okay, so in terms of our micro frontend design principles, how do micro apps as an approach to micro frontends score? So in terms of each one of our micro apps being an autonomous feature, we score well. Each micro app can be independently changed and deployed and the code is completely isolated, because it is an independent application. And in terms of communication between our micro apps, we can achieve communication between our micro apps by using links between each application, links which feature, for example, query string parameters in order to communicate certain information between each application, or we can use microservices in the background as a way of each one of our micro apps sharing data behind the scenes. We also score well in terms of team ownership. Because it is a separate app with its own code, with its own code repository, a team can own the entire micro app end to end. So, by end to end we mean that the team can own not only the micro application, but also the microservices and the data stores which empower our micro application in the background infrastructure. We also score well in terms of having our micro frontend as technology agnostic. Because each micro app is completely physically separate from all our other applications, we can use any technology for the micro frontend application and we can use any technologies for the backend services and data stores that enable that micro application. Now where things go slightly wrong for our micro apps approach as an approach to micro frontend architecture, is under the user experience design principle. For example, although we can give the illusion of having one unified application, there are limitations to that illusion. So, for example, in our shopping website example, if I want to have a quick peek at my shopping basket in terms of what have I already bought, what I've already placed into my shopping basket, it will be a little bit unusual if I need to move away from my current product page and move onto a separate page, a separate micro app which actually shows me the shopping basket. And like this example, there will be many other use case scenarios where I want all my micro frontend applications to actually appear on the same page or on the same screen at the same time. And overall this will lead to a poor UI flow, and it forces the user to become the integration mechanism between your micro applications because they are having to jump between different micro apps for different parts of your application, so this is the main disadvantages of micro apps as an approach to micro frontends architecture. To gain technical modularity in terms of micro frontends, we are slightly ruining the user experience in terms of usability of our unified application. And as previously mentioned, there are different ways of trying to reinforce the illusion of one application, and achieving the best user experience still can be challenging. In terms of the other design principles, each one of our micro apps can still be value driven. End to end, each micro app can be designed to deliver one specific feature to the customer in a very optimized way because we control the entire end to end architecture in terms of frontend microservices and data storage. And as we've mentioned before, each one of these micro apps can have its own set of dedicated microservices which empower the application, and the micro app basically becomes an extension of specific functionality provided by microservices within the background. In the next section of this module, we will look at how iframes can be used as a technology to create micro frontends architecture.

Iframes

Another web technology that can be used to implement micro frontend architecture is known as iframes, and iframes as an approach falls under the same category as micro apps, in that they run in a separate runtime when running your micro frontend applications. And this, again, means there are fewer conflicts between our micro frontend applications in terms of shared resources where overlapping variables and versioning issues are an issue between frameworks and libraries,

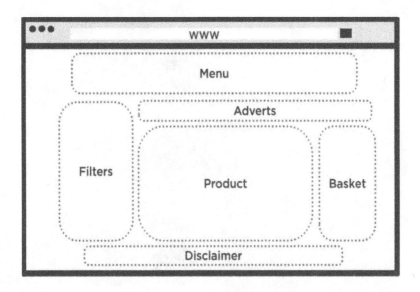

and the key advantage that iframes provide over micro apps is the ability to have all our micro frontend applications on one web page, and overall providing a better illusion of having one unified application. The key disadvantage is that it is a web-based technology, and for mobile applications you would have to use something like PhoneGap in order to have a mobile application that actually uses web-based technology.

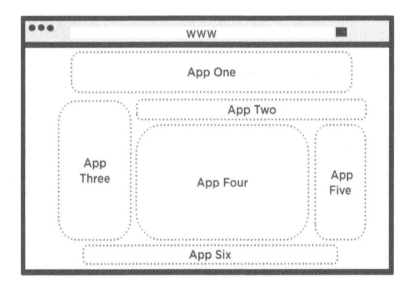

And like micro apps, each one of our micro frontend applications within an iframe is actually an independent application,

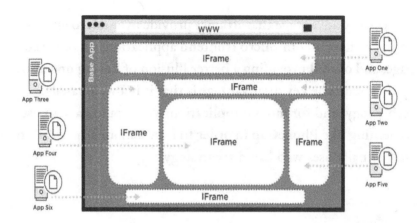

an independent application that can be loaded from any web
server that's hosting that application into an iframe, an iframe that
sits within a main base application, a base HTML page.

> Autonomous Features ✔
> Team Ownership ✔
> Tech Agnostic ✔
> User Experience ✘
> Value Driven ✔
> Microservice Driven ✔

In terms of micro frontend architecture design principles, the good news is our iframe-based micro frontends are completely autonomous. Each micro frontend is basically an application that's embedded within an iframe and is completely encapsulated, which means each one of our iframe-based micro frontend applications can be independently changed and deployed without breaking any one of our other micro frontend applications. The bad news is, it's very difficult to share resources with the base application and other iframe-based applications. You would have to have a centralized CDN type of system if you want to share resources which are UI related. And in order for your micro frontend applications to talk to each other, within an iframe you can either use the Windows events, raise events from your iframe, then pick up those events by other iframe-based applications, or you can have microservices in the background talking to each other, enabling communication between your micro frontend applications. And also, in terms of team ownership we are still good because your team can still own that micro frontend application end to end, because within the iframe it is basically a micro app that's running within that iframe, and you can own that end to end in terms of backend microservices and the storage associated with those microservices. Basically, one team can deliver an entire feature in the form of an iframe micro frontend end to end, and because of the separate runtime for an iframe-based micro frontend applications, each one of our micro frontend applications can still be technology agnostic. We can basically use a different framework, for example, a JavaScript framework for each one of our micro frontend applications, because they are completely encapsulated within each one of the iframes. A separate runtime basically ensures there are no conflicts between the frameworks in terms of framework types and versions, and there's no naming issues in terms of variables across the global space within the web application. Another thing that makes iframes a reliable option for micro frontend applications is the fact that they are such a mature technology, and browser support across the board is pretty much 100%, although user experience with iframe-based micro frontend applications is better than the micro apps option primarily due to the fact that all our micro frontend applications can be on the same page, i. e., the same screen. There is, however, a risk to user experience if we have any sizing issues within one of our micro frontend applications. You might start seeing scroll bars appear around the iframe. Another area of concern for iframe-based micro frontend applications is performance. If we end up with several micro frontends on the screen, each with their own separate runtime, and each with their own separate JavaScript framework loaded into the memory, we might end up with performance issues. And because there is this risk of creating a resource heavy application because of the separate runtimes and resource usages, it's important to test your application in terms of performance to guarantee user experience. On the plus side, iframe-based micro frontend applications allow us to deliver value better than micro applications, because all our micro frontend applications are on the same screen, and we still can individually develop each iframe-based micro frontend application end to end to deliver a specific function and a specific value to the customer. And because each iframe within our micro frontends architecture will feature a micro application, a micro application which is basically an extension of specific functionality in our backend infrastructure, basically an extension of a microservice, and therefore, iframe-based micro frontends still allow us to extend microservices architecture from the backend to the frontend. In the next section of this module, we will start looking at the use of web components as a way of delivering micro frontends architecture.

Web Components

In this section, we will discuss another web-based technology called web components that can help us implement our micro frontends architecture, and each one of our micro frontend applications is basically implemented using a web component on an HTML page, and all this is done using a shared runtime environment. And this basically means the global space of our web app is shared between the web components, and therefore, memory and resources are shared across the web components. Although this sounds like the opposite of what we want, there is a form of encapsulation which is provided by web components for our micro frontend applications which we will explain later on.

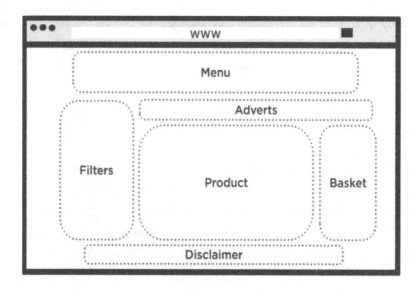

And like iframes, web components allow us to have our micro frontend applications work together on one page, on one screen.

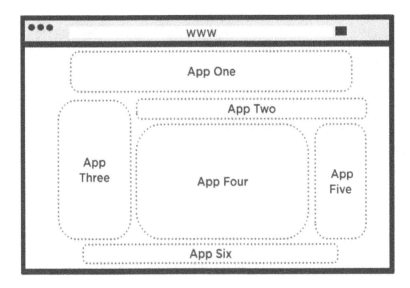

Each one of our micro frontend applications is basically rendered on the HTML page as a web component,

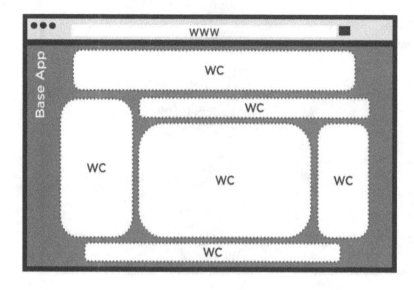

and the contents of each web component can live on any web app server, and it can be served into this one application in the form of a web component.

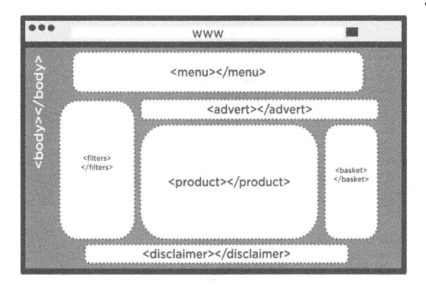

In terms of HTML, each micro frontend application, i. e., each web component, is basically a custom HTML element which sits within the base apps HTML.

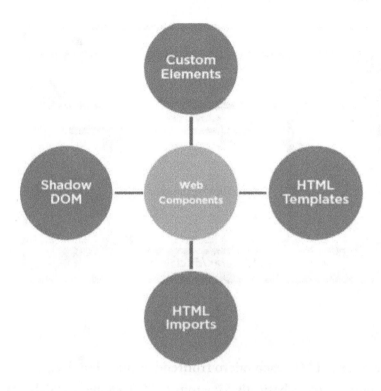

- ➢ Encapsulation
- ➢ Framework agnostic component model
- ➢ Series of W3C standards
    - ○ Custom elements
    - ○ HTML templates
    - ○ Shadow DOM
    - ○ HTML imports
- ➢ Micro frontends as custom elements
- ➢ Polyfills and support libraries
- ➢ Browser as an API
- ➢ Web app or mobile hybrid app

And the basic idea is these empty-looking custom elements provide encapsulation to the content that they render as part of our main application. And the best thing about web components is that they are not tied to a specific JavaScript framework, they are actually built using bog-standard HTML, CSS, and JavaScript, and in reality it's not one standard, it's not one web standard that defines how these native web components work, it's actually a number of web standards that work together to enable web components. The first standard that we will discuss which help build web components is something known as the custom element standard, and this standard allows you to create custom elements, HTML elements, that your browser recognizes. It also allows you to extend existing HTML elements. So, for example, for the product micro frontend with a new application, so the mini application which displays the product within your shopping website, you would use the custom element standard to define a custom element which represents that micro frontend. So, for example, we would have a custom element called product, and the custom element standard works along with the HTML template standard, and this standard, the HTML template standard, is used to define the contents of your micro frontend application, and the HTML template is associated with the custom element, and therefore, when the browser comes across the custom element, it uses the HTML template to render your micro frontend application. And the magical part of web components is in the form of a standard called the Shadow DOM standard, and it's this standard that allows the encapsulation of our micro frontend application within the web component by allowing us to encapsulate the DOM and the Starling within our web component. And what this means is the contents of our micro frontend application, i. e., the HTML, the DOM, the Starling, and the JavaScript associated with our micro frontend application lives within this web component in an encapsulated fashion, in that it works independently from everything else. And although we are still running our application within the shared runtime, we almost have all the advantages of having a separate runtime because the Shadow DOM almost mimics that environment, so our web components more or less work like iframes. And it's the HTML import standard which allows us to have different web components imported into different applications, so we could have our micro frontend application defined as a web component, and using an HTML import statement we can import this into a specific web page.

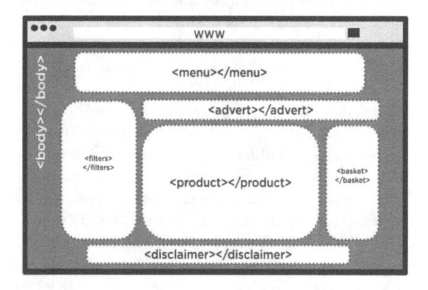

And all these standards work together, allowing us to have our micro frontends defined as custom elements, custom elements that we can import into any part of our application using these standards. And although web components use native web standards, the support across some specific browsers for web components and some of these standards is still a bit weak. The good news is there are a number of polyfills and support libraries that are available that ensure your micro frontend applications work consistently as web components across all web browsers.

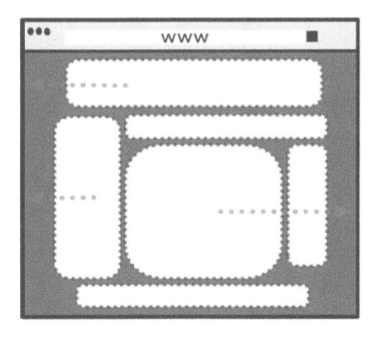

And because these custom elements that represent your web components are still part of the main DOM, you can use the browser as an API in terms of the web components communicating with each other. You can still raise events and do stuff at a browser level, which allows the communication between the web components.

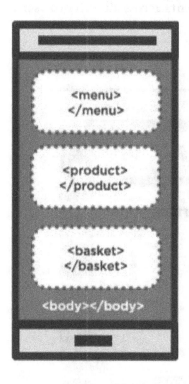

And although web components is a web standard that can be easily used within mobile applications where the mobile application is a hybrid application using technologies like PhoneGap,

- ➢ Autonomous Features ✔
- ➢ Team Ownership ✔
- ➢ Tech Agnostic ✔
- ➢ User Experience ✔
- ➢ Value Driven ✔
- ➢ Microservice Driven ✔

and in terms of micro frontend architecture design principles, web components score really well. Thanks to the shadow DOM and the HTML template standard, web components can be developed as autonomous features that can be independently changed and deployed without affecting the rest of the application. And because we have this encapsulated area, i. e., the web component in the form of a Shadow DOM, the teams can own each one of their micro frontend applications end to end. The can own the HTML and the contents that's loaded into the web component and makes up the Shadow DOM and the HTML template. And also, because of the encapsulation, we can also use any technology we want within our web components because it's encapsulated from the rest of the application, allowing us to develop our micro frontend application within a web component which, for example, uses Angular, and we could develop another separate one which sits on the same page as a custom element, but this time the web component uses something like React within the micro frontend web component. The key advantage that web components have over iframes is user experience. This is all to do with the sizing of our micro frontend application. If we have sizing issues within our iframe-based micro frontend application, there's a possibility we might see scroll bars within our application around our micro frontend application, whereas with the web component version, our micro frontend application is still rendered as an element within the parent DOM, and therefore, if there is a sizing issue, the parent DOM will adjust accordingly. Although web components give us so many advantages, we've still got to be sensible in terms of how we use them. For example, if we start loading different frameworks within each one of our web components, our application can overall become resource heavy. Therefore, we need to be really sensible in terms of how many frameworks we use across our micro frontend applications, and that we test for performance. And because web components allow us to create small enough micro frontend applications which are embedded within an overall unified application, we can bring specific features to the customer which provide the customer value. And although our micro frontend application will look like a simple custom element when implemented as web components, in the background there can be a range of microservices which empower that specific web component, i. e., a specific micro frontend application. Basically, the HTML associated with that specific web component will make calls using JavaScript or whatever framework it's using to backend microservices which are specifically for that micro frontend application. In the next section of the module, we will look at another type of component which allows micro frontend applications. These are components which are based around, or are from, specific JavaScript frameworks.

Framework Based Components

Okay, so in this section of the module we will look at how framework-based components can be used for micro frontend architecture. And this is a very similar approach to web components in terms of containing your micro frontend application within a component which sits within your web application.

> Angular.js
> React.js
> Vue.js

> JavaScript frameworks
> Need for components
> Enable micro frontends
> Realized the need for web components
> Challenges
>> ○ Vendor lock-in
>> ○ Web components better option
>> ○ Difficult to migrate
>> ○ Combining multiple frameworks

And it's clear to see the main creators of the major JavaScript frameworks like Angular, like Vue, like React, saw the need for a modular frontend,

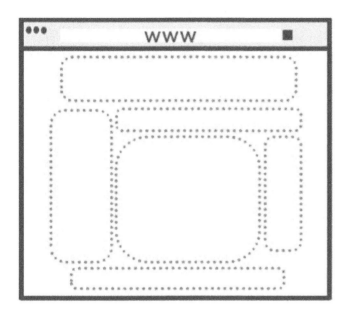

whilst standards around native web components were still being finalized, and this is why you find component architecture is the core part of the JavaScript frameworks.

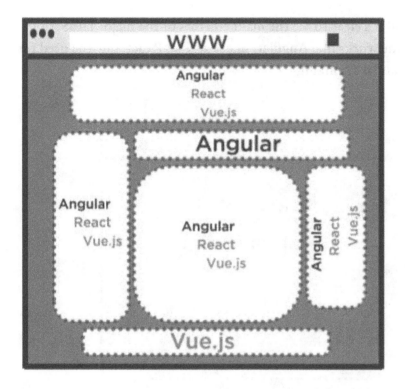

It's the ability to encapsulate parts of your frontend application into independent components which is what enables our micro frontends architecture. And this framework-based implementation for component architecture, for micro frontend architecture, realizes the long-term need for standard native web components which enable micro frontend architecture. And right now these framework-based components have huge support from the community and from large vendors. And because of this support, if I want to create an enterprise-level application it's easy to use a framework-based architecture using a popular JavaScript framework, because it already provides that modularity in terms of supporting micro frontend architecture. Obviously strategy and processes will need to be put in place to ensure your use of framework-based components encourages the micro frontend architecture design principles. This, for example, might include if, for example, you're using Angular as a base framework, how you allocate your micro frontend applications to a team in the form of a component, how you source control those components, and how you keep them separate in order to encourage the micro frontend design principles.

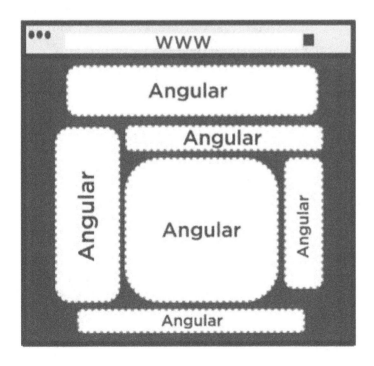

There are, however, challenges associated with relying on a framework for your component architecture to enable micro frontends. The first obvious one is you are investing in that framework in order to provide a base architecture for your micro frontend architecture, so therefore you're kind of almost locked into that JavaScript framework, whereas the native web components option you're using native web standards in order to implement your component architecture, and therefore, you're not really locked into a specific JavaScript framework. And the main problem with investing into a specific framework is, over time it will become more and more difficult to migrate to anything new. And historically we've seen over time that even large frameworks from reputable vendors often get replaced. There are many companies out there who initially invested heavily within, for example, Angular version 1, and then as that turned into AngularJS, there's now a need to migrate the AngularJS applications into Angular in order to ensure that there's long-term support. So long term, if you invest too heavily into one framework, long term eventually you'll need a migration strategy, and that migration strategy might be very painful because you've heavily invested in the component architecture of a specific framework,

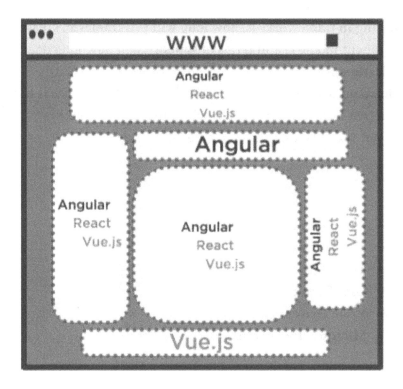

and so by investing heavily into one framework, you lose the ability to use multiple frameworks at the same time. So, for example, if you want to experiment with React and Angular at the same time, you might lose that advantage. Having said that, there are other frameworks out there which try and give you base architecture which allows you to combine different JavaScript frameworks. But this raises the question, are you investing in another base framework for your architecture to enable the ability to use multiple different frameworks? Again, long term this might not be a good idea. The overall question you need to ask when investing in frameworks is, how long will this framework-based component model last in terms of support, and how long does my application need to last? It's very difficult for a business to understand why an entire enterprise-level application needs to be re-written just because a little detail in the background has changed and that a framework is no longer supported.

➤ Autonomous Features ✗
➤ Team Ownership ✔
➤ Tech Agnostic ✗
➤ User Experience ✔
➤ Value Driven ✔
➤ Microservice Driven ✔

Okay, now let's quickly have a look at how framework-based components for a micro frontend architecture do in terms of satisfying the design principles for micro frontend architecture. Okay, so the first question is, do framework-based components encourage micro frontends, which are autonomous features? And I had kind of a 50/50 feeling on this. Although you can use components in isolation in terms of source controlling them separately to the rest of the micro frontend applications, which make your entire application, can you really independently change them? Can you really independently deploy them when changing them and deploying them actually requires heavy integration back into the base application? So, for example, if we're using Angular and Angular components, if I change a certain component and introduce new services, I need to integrate all of this stuff, again, back into the base application, which means my base application has also changed, and I might accidentally introduce a change which affects another component, another micro frontend which is also registered within the same base application. And also, what if the base framework itself changes in terms of versions? Will I need to update all of my components so that they match the same version, for example, if there's a syntax change? And this will mean updating all your micro frontend applications and then integrating them back into the base application. So framework-based components are autonomous to a certain extent, but not completely. In terms of team ownership, we are okay because our micro frontend applications in the form of framework-based components can be packaged separately into files and source controlled, and they can be owned by a specific team, and specific teams can then control exactly how that component, that micro frontend application interacts with specific backend microservices and data stores that they own. And we've already mentioned the fact that these frameworks don't really encourage our micro frontend applications to be technology agnostic. At a technical level, these frameworks might be well documented and supported, and supported across several different browsers, but they do lock you into that specific framework. You in the main lose the ability to try different different frameworks and technologies for your different micro frontend applications that make up your whole application. From a user experience point of view, with framework-based components we're in a good place, and most of this component architecture is well optimized for the framework that they are built around. And if you do choose to invest just in one framework, the browser only has to load that one framework for your entire micro frontend application, because all your micro frontend applications will work off the same framework, so there is definitely a performance gain there. There are some frameworks which are slightly heavier than other frameworks in terms of the number of files required and that kind of stuff to be downloaded in order for the framework to work as an application. The other advantage of using framework-based components is the flexibility they give you. So not only can I have my micro frontend applications all on the same application, giving the illusion of one application, but I can have micro frontend applications embedded within micro frontend applications, so you can have components which are made up of components, which again, might give you flexibility for those niche scenarios where that's required. Another thing that improves user experience is the reliability of some of these frameworks. The large vendors who support some of these JavaScript frameworks go out of their way to make sure that the frameworks work consistently across different browsers, and this overall improves the user experience. And in terms of value-driven micro frontend applications, we are still good, because we can bring these components to our application, which bring a specific feature that brings value to our customer in an end-to-end fashion. So not only can we modularize our micro frontend application by encapsulating within this component, that component can be optimized in terms of end-to-end infrastructure in terms of having optimized microservices in the background to support its functionality. And which leads to the final point, which is framework-based components still allow us to extend our microservices architecture in that components can be designed to surface the functionality of specific microservices in the background so you can have an end-to-end solution where you have a component, a micro frontend which is an extension to a microservice or a set of microservices in your background infrastructure. Okay, so in the next section of this module, we'll look at how something called transclusion can be used as a way of delivering micro frontend architecture.

Transclusion

Okay, so in this final section of the module we will look at another set of techniques and technologies which fall under a category called transclusion, and this category covers a number of techniques and technologies that can help develop a micro frontends architecture. And there are two key categories, subcategories of transclusion when applied as a solution to micro frontends architecture.

- ➢ Apps rendered at server side
- ➢ Edge side includes
- ➢ Various tech to do server side rendering
- ➢ Multiple apps delivered as a page
- ➢ Pros
  - ○ Simplifies client side processing
  - ○ User experience
- ➢ Cons
  - ○ Slows overall page
  - ○ No native way of doing
- ➢ Browser includes content using AJAX
- ➢ hinclude.js and h-include.js
- ➢ Multiple apps delivered as a page
- ➢ There are alternative ways
- ➢ Pros
  - ○ No need for backend complexity

➢ Cons
  ○ Frontend complexity
  ○ Frontend performance

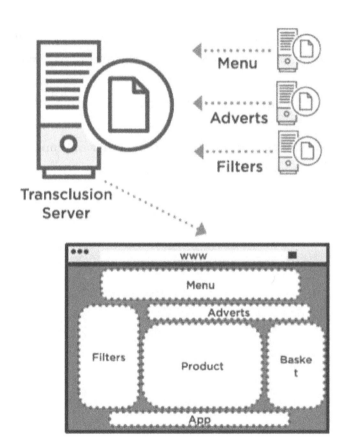

You can have server-side transclusion, which is what we'll start off with, and you can also have client-side transclusion, which we'll cover later on. And the idea behind transclusion overall is pretty straightforward. Your application is still made up of many other applications and is rendered as one application, as one screen, so your one screen can consist of many micro frontend applications, but these micro frontend applications are brought together at the server-side when using server-side transclusion. There's basically an engine running server-side which forms the overall page which is sent back to the browser, and that engine basically constructs that page by using sources from other applications, from other different application servers, and it brings the contents from each one of those applications and brings them together into one page, which is then pre-rendered and sent to the browser.

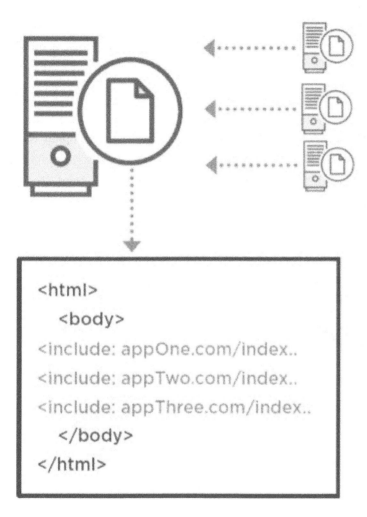

And an example of a standard, a web standard which enables this is called Edge Side Includes, sometimes known as ESI. And this standard basically suggests to include tags within your HTML pages, which allow you to bring contents from different servers. So these might be different servers with their own web apps, and the contents of the web apps can be included in this central page by using ESI include tags, and there's an ESI processor or an ESI engine running on a central server which picks up all the include tags and then goes away and fetches the contents, and then replaces the tags with the content. And then the final page sent back to the client, the client application, is the fully rendered page, including all the several different applications or several different pages that make up that one overall page.

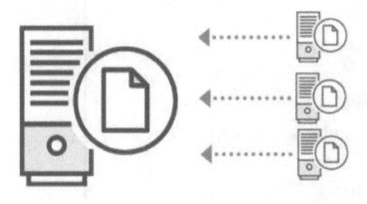

And there are many frameworks out there that try and implement the ESI standard and provide a form of this engine, which pre-renders the page and delivers it to your browser.

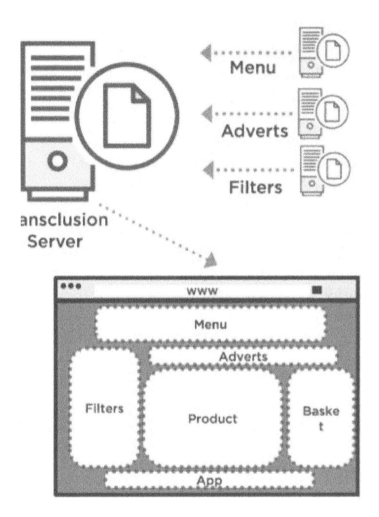

But the overall idea is straightforward. Your micro frontend applications run in the background on different web servers, and it's the ESI engine or the transclusion server-side engine which then brings all the contents from each one of your micro frontend applications together into one page. And there are a few advantages to this approach when used for micro frontends architecture. It simplifies the client-side processing, so what's delivered to your browser is fairly straightforward. There is no sign of a heavyweight framework which is trying to do everything at the client side. And because of this lightweight application running within the browser as a web app, the overall user experience also improves, because the complexity of bringing these multiple micro frontends together is kind of already handled server side by the transclusion engine. There are also some disadvantages. If not done properly at the server-side end in terms of performance, it can slow the delivery of the page to the browser. If your transclusion engine is taking forever to bring your micro frontend applications together into one unified application or page, there might be a bit of a lag before the content is delivered to the browser. The other disadvantage is currently there is no native way of actually doing this. There is no engine built into Windows servers or Linux servers which allows transclusion for this type of purpose. You'll have to use some kind of third-party software to act as a transclusion engine.

AJAX

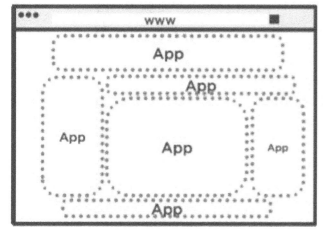

It's also possible to do transclusion at the client side, and this is where your web application, your base app, will use technologies like AJAX to pull down your micro frontend applications from different servers onto one page to give the illusion of one application.

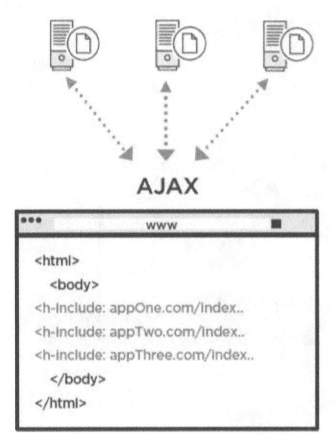

There are a number of JavaScript libraries out there which will allow you to perform transclusion within your web pages, and the idea is pretty much exactly the same. You include a bunch of include tags within your base application, and each one of these include tags is configured to talk to backend servers in order to pull content down,

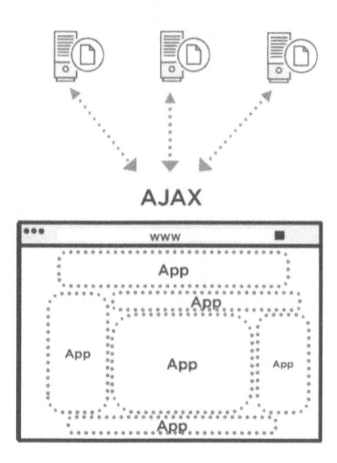

i. e., to pull your micro frontend application down into a specific part of the base application. There are other native technologies and standards available that do a similar thing in terms of bringing content into tags included into your base application. So, for example, on this course we have previously mentioned things like web components and iframes, which might do things slightly differently, but the end result is very similar. It is pulling content from different places to make this one unified application. One of the advantages of client-side transclusion is that unlike server-side transclusion you don't need backend systems and backend engines to perform the transclusion at the backend level, so the backend architecture is slightly simplified in terms of the infrastructure required. The disadvantages for client-side transclusion should be fairly obvious. We've taken the complexity from the backend system and we've brought the complexity to the frontend part of our application. Our frontend application now basically relies on third-party libraries to perform the transclusion and to construct our overall application by pulling the micro frontend applications down. Another obvious disadvantage we need to worry about is performance at the client-side application end. If our applications, if our frontend micro apps take different times to load, how long will it take for the overall page to render completely? Will we find inconsistencies in terms of rendering different parts of the application, different micro frontends which make up our overall application? Will there be a difference in speed in terms of rendering specific micro frontend applications?

- ➢ Autonomous Features ✔
- ➢ Team Ownership ✔
- ➢ Tech Agnostic ✗
- ➢ User Experience ✗
- ➢ Value Driven ✔
- ➢ Microservice Driven ✔

Now let's have a quick look at how transclusion satisfies our micro frontend architecture design principles. And because our micro frontend applications are running in the background on servers as independent apps that are pulled down either at server side using server-side transclusion or at client side using client-side transclusion, our micro frontend applications are still independently deployable and changeable, and therefore, they are still autonomous features, because they are independent encapsulated apps which are pulled down either client side or server side into one overall page. And because they are independent encapsulated applications, our micro frontend applications, a team can easily own them end to end. So they can own the micro frontend application which is pulled down into a page as a component which works end to end with microservices and data stores which empower it, so you can have a team own that complete vertical slice off that micro frontend application. In terms of making our micro frontend applications technology agnostic, the result is kind of 50/50, in that I might be able to use any technology I want to use for my micro frontend application, but that technology needs to play well with our transclusion technology. So, for example, if I'm using Angular for one of my micro frontend applications, can my transclusion engine, either server-side or client-side, can it render my micro frontend application correctly as part of the transclusion engine's process to create this illusion of one unified application? The other concern with transclusion in terms of technology is, are we locked into a specific framework which provides the transclusion, and long term, if support dies for this framework, we will need to do a migration from one transclusion engine to another transclusion engine, and at the same time we'll have to assess each one of our micro frontend applications to ensure that they are still compatible with the new transclusion engine. And the user experience is still a concern, because if we're using server-side transclusion, if the pre-rendering of the server end is delayed, will it delay the delivery of our application to the browser, and then ruining the user's experience? And then with client-side transclusion there's a concern if we're transcluding at the client side on our client side's page within the web application, will it actually slow the web page down because it's pulling all these micro frontend applications from servers in the background using a third-party library? In terms of value-driven micro frontend application, we are still okay because our app is still encapsulated as an independent application on a server in the background somewhere, and we can have this owned by a team, and they can develop and optimize this end to end from the frontend application to the services and the data storage in the background, all optimized to bring value to the customer and to be included within our overall application. And this, again, highlights the fact that there's nothing with this solution with transclusion that hinders us from using our microservices architecture in the background. We can still use our micro frontend applications as independent applications that are an extension of the functionality that the microservices expose in the background.

Summary

- ➤ Separate Runtime
    - ○ Micro Apps
    - ○ Iframes
- ➤ Shared Runtime
    - ○ Web Components
    - ○ Framework Based Components
    - ○ Transclusion

Okay, so in this module we've looked at different techniques and technologies which enable us to create a micro frontend architecture. And we started off by looking at techniques and technologies that fall under the category of separate runtime, and these techniques and technologies from micro apps to iframes, run your micro frontend applications in complete isolation from each other. And we then moved onto looking at techniques and technologies that run your micro frontend applications within a shared runtime, and although having a shared runtime can be seen as a disadvantage, each one of these technologies had its own means of negating those disadvantages and isolating your micro apps into its own encapsulated component. And under this category we looked at the different types of component implementations that are available to make your micro frontends a reality from native web components to framework-based components. And then we concluded the module by looking at a different approach to building up an application made up of micro frontends by looking at something called server-side transclusion and client-side transclusion, and how they brought your micro frontend applications together to create one unified application. Hopefully from this module, and from this course overall, you can see that it's quite clear what we want to achieve in terms of micro frontend architecture in terms of the advantages we want to gain from such architecture, but there are several different ways of implementing this architecture using different techniques and technologies.

www.ingramcontent.com/pod-product-compliance
Lightning Source LLC
Chambersburg PA
CBHW071223050326
40689CB00011B/2431